STALKINC

# Stalking Paloma

IFOR THOMAS

Parthian
The Old Surgery
Napier Street
Cardigan
SA43 1ED
www.parthianbooks.com

First published in 2011
© Ifor Thomas
All Rights Reserved

ISBN 978-1-908069-66-5

Cover painting by Warren Williams
Back cover photo by Dom Atreides Stocqueler
Typesetting: www.littlefishpress.com
Printed and bound by Gwasg Gomer, Llandysul, Wales

Published with the financial support of the Welsh Books Council.

Privacy is dead

Mark Zuckerberg, Founder of *Facebook*

For Gill

# Contents

# Stalking Paloma

# Feed me

RB-7JJT3-FT6SC-FEBPS-VXGM2-XUB9K-4ANRX

You are viewing a feed that contains frequently updated content. When you subscribe to a feed, it is added to the Common Feed List. Updated information from the feed is automatically downloaded to your computer and can be viewed in Internet Explorer and other programs.

*Does anyone know any backline techs that would like a day's work tomorrow? London-based, must be able to drive a splitter...*

# Apollo

You are ready to go
standing on the heart-shaped
white grand piano
your wings snap open
green dress
red hair
dragonfly
hovering on a thermal
of adoration

Into your set
mosh pit churning
a stricken monster
sound so loud it compresses air
reverberates up my spine
hunts out the spleen
fills the skull
fiery gasoline

Appropriate this venue
The Hammersmith Apollo
God of music
poetry and
get this
plague
I should know

# Birds

Two peewits cry
for the cormorant in his funeral silk
lapwings abandon the lowlands
on the long flight of bone
a fist of starlings punches the sky

Jays and goldcrests, rare red kites
eagles have their place
tern, gull and the restless wader
a kingfisher watcher
dipper walking, owl in the lights

The hawk's deadly sight
peregrine takes the woodcock
the corner of the cock's lizard eye
rooks with black breasts
a pair of swans poised for flight

The charmed kestrel words
her neck a swan's curve
green woodpecker flies
for three weeks the albatross roads
plotting our escape like jail birds

*Sampled from Poetry 1900 – 2000*
*One hundred poets from Wales*

# I follow you

I follow you on twitter weigh your every tweet, 140 characters, haiku for our digital age. Your life story, this one post your War and Peace

# Playing chess with Osama bin Laden

I used to play chess with Osama bin Laden,
although for the purpose
he called himself NoBamaYoMomma.

We hooked up every day.
He was better than me, but arrogant.
He sacrificed pieces with gay abandon.

His moves arrived in the middle of the night.
My iPhone bleeping in the dark
as he opened a front on my Queen side flank.

He usually won with a move of the bishop,
rook or whatever piece was left
after the carnage. Occasionally he lost,

but only, I guess, because he was distracted
by the latest developments in the global jihad,
or some detail like the poor quality

of suicide bodybelt buckles.
In our last game I offered him a draw
which he contemplated

in a bedroom of the high-walled house,
his wife turning her head
to the sound of approaching helicopters.

# Mercury

I listen as the shortlist is announced:
Dizzee Rascal's *Tongue N' Cheek*,
Biffy Clyro's *Only Revolutions*
Mumford & Sons' debut *Sigh No More*
The xx, Laura Marling, Villagers,
I Am Kloot, Foals
and Wild Beasts.
Paul Weller's *Wake Up the Nation*.
Later, you tweet bravely.
But you and I both know
This is a terrible injustice.

# Getting Mills into the car

I have put the seat back as far as it will go.
Still he struggles to manoeuvre his bulk
into what now appears like something
     made miniature.
Once in, he cannot lean out to shut the door.

When he was much thinner,
and surprisingly attractive to beautiful women,
he filled my life more.

At the reunion event
he remembers the name of a woman
I had long since forgotten,
perhaps because he had slept with her
and she, in the middle of it all,
had burst into tears,
crying for her greatest love.

Now after twenty years
she eyes his bulk in wonderment,
then turns to me,
asks after Nigel.

# What to say when criticising poetry
## (like this poem)

The title's good
*(I can't think of anything to say about this poem)*

Can you read it again?
*(Give me time please to think of something to say)*

It's too long
*(Never: it's too short)*

Lose the last line
*(And the rest of it, for all I care)*

The idea behind the poem is much better than the poem
  itself
*(Although that's not saying much)*

I like your new approach to language
*(Are you dyslexic?)*

Some of your images are truly memorable
*(Whose poem have you ripped off?)*

Isn't this two poems in one?
*(It's a mish-mash)*

I need to read this on the page
*(It's too dense, like the poet)*

You really read your poetry well
*(But you write like an arsehole)*

Have you thought about your audience?
*(This poem is therapy – see a psychiatrist)*

You could place this somewhere
*(Like the bin)*

It's a new approach to an old theme
*(It's a clichéd mess)*

It's a good performance piece
*(It's crap)*

Have you thought about putting the last line first?
*(Like this poem)*

# He planted trees

Through the seasons
she watched them grow
pulled high by light
swollen with rain
kneaded by wind

Now he has gone
leaving only the long handled axe
that leans by the shed door
like a nonchalant lover

# The business of bone

Shadow of cloud is
a medieval map of the world
projected by autumn sun
onto the escarpment of Pen y Fan

even to the whale
that spouts a white plume
of scattered sheep into the green yonder
a moving mass of misplaced forestry

I guess an observer there
looking across at us
could have the same thought
we sift space between shifting continents

our business is bone
and healing after the accident
that cracked her vertebra like a cold twig
on this snow covered slope

we cannot decide where the sledge
catapulted her into casualty
and a New Year's Eve on Ward 1
throwing up as fireworks splattered the sky

consigned to her carapace
through the unbending months of winter
in her whale-boned corsetry
she cut a dash in Sainsbury's

she is picking through other bones
in a nest of wool a sheep's skeleton
arranges itself haphazardly
it too a victim of chance disaster

skull broken unzipped fragments
only the teeth solid in their sockets
gritted against the wind
which shears the slope

she studies these remains
counting vertebrae
beads of a broken rosary
through it all she kept the faith

she looks away and down
at the bikers bright as dragonflies
burning up the mountain road
the wind blows the world changes

# Eyeing the Merc

Glyn's fucked off to Spain,
split with his wife,
quit the Crystals.
His old E-class remains
settling into the car park bay.

A veteran of booze and baccy runs
filled to the gunwhales with
Belgian Old Holborn handrolling
French health warnings –
it now grows ferns from the doors
moss on the rubber gaskets.

The Merc star has long gone
otherwise it's only moderately vandalised,
the *this car has no tax and will be taken away*
   notice
has disappeared without trace.

Steve's missus has to squeeze her Nissan
into the space next to the Merc.
It gets his goat – someday
somebody will torch the bastard.
I tell him to call the council,
get the crate shifted – it drags down the estate.
Steve shakes his head,
goes against the grain
to connive with authority.

So we stand here,
Sunday morning,
eyeing the Merc,
he tells me
of his second
vasectomy.

# Stalking Paloma

The hard disc spins,
and we meet again, Paloma.
My hot hand on the remote
– slo-mo, freeze frame, fast forward.
How many ways can I watch you?

Tonight I have time.
Let my gaze linger on
the stars that stud your steepling cheeks,
eyelids glittering butterflies,
lips returning the microphone's kiss.

I deconstruct your cubist dress
as you raise your arms above your crown.
The backing singers sway,
weed in the roaring river of your beauty.
You teetering on those outrageous blue heels.

The band, loose drummer, louche bassist:
too-good guitar player, all flotsam
in the wake of your soaring vocals.
Electronic pulses tattoo my cortex,
images fold and flash like sunlight.

The music stops. That smile.
You give it just to me.
I press pause,
pin you to my imagination.
Freeze us.

# Now that you have gone

I cook food you like
although you are not here to eat it.
I heat the house
even though I prefer it cold.

I wake at the time you would
and that's later than I'm used to.
When I open my eyes
I see what you saw,

because I sleep
on your side of the bed.
On websites
I trace your month in phone calls,

watch the ebb and flow of your money,
list the hotels you have stayed at,
the meals you have eaten.
Your gym visits

have increased exponentially:
obviously, you are in good shape.
On Google Earth
I hover over you like an angel.

Your music is on my iPod,
and I'm slowly reading
your favourite novel,
curled up in what was your chair.

I have taken to wearing
your perfume to remind me
of how you smell.
Your underwear is next to my skin.

Tomorrow, I will kill your lover.
On the chopping board,
the one you brought me from Vietnam,
I will mince your lover's heart,

feed it to your cat,
who is not getting
the attention she deserves,
now that you have gone.

# Baked Bass

He talks of lost love,
of a wife of thirty years
sleeping with his best friend, her
his child bride.

He's like a teenager,
this middle-aged man.
His eyes blur, there's not
a day he hasn't cried.

I invent infidelities of my own –
men, women, blow-up dolls
have all featured in my ruinous love life.
There's nothing I haven't tried.

*She took you back?*
He removes his glasses to eat,
this wet afternoon in Bridgend.
*She took me back*. I lied.

We share a baked bass,
the waiter cracks its salt shell,
unpicks skin and bones.
My friend considers suicide.

His phone flashes a text,
I read it, as he cannot see
*I'm going away,*
*I'm happy, but terrified.*

*I love you Ken,*
*but I love him more.*
He looks at me, says,
*It's as if I'm being bribed*

*With sweet words*
*To mask her betrayal,*
*She thinks I'm stupid*
*She treats me like a child.*

So the rain falls.
I try to be practical.
*Make sure access*
*to your money is denied.*

*Starve out the bitch.*
*Change the locks.*
*Engage a solicitor.*
*Don't get mired*

*in self-pity, loathing.*
But his mind has gone.
*I think, he contemplates his fate –*
*I would have preferred this fish fried.*

# Blossom Falling

I remember spring in Kyoto.
In the Imperial Palace gardens
blossom was falling.

I think of the palace guide.
With no common tongue
we sculpted words out of air.

Now the doctor places
pictures in front of me,
pictures of animals for children.

*What are these animals called?*
I see blossom falling,
I see the trees denied their glory.

Whiteness of blossom,
a stone bridge over still water,
sound of my feet on raked gravel.

Then, in the failed fuse board,
wires connect – *Cow, dog*
I say as if I'd known all along.

*What of the other?* He asks.
Waiting, watching, writing.
My bird has flown,

leaving only lines, colour on paper.

# Good time

Others might think me a loner
sat in the corner of the bar,
iPhone buds plugged into my ears,
but you and I know different.
I'm reading your tweets
listening to your voice –
eye on the door.

I half expect you to walk in.
This pub is where
I went after the first
of many gigs.

I know you have seen me,
not jumping around with the rest of them
but watching, listening to the lyrics
of songs especially for me:
you always look in my direction and smile.

Sometimes I stand outside your apartment block,
watch the lights, know you are looking back at
    me,
wondering whether to come down and let me in.

Do you tell your friends about me?
For now
I'm going to let this love grow,
then I'm coming to get you,
rescue you from your life,
show you a really good time.

# Birthday boy

Autumn on my tongue,
sharp as barely-ripe apples,
this morning deserves better
than me, the birthday boy.
A squirrel runs, climbs –
taking the piss, I'd say.
My Boxfresh, running feet;
might as well be wearing
diver's boots, pounding to
the toll of another bell.

Sand-churned sea
ripped by waves,
the tide runs against itself
and me. One more time
through the wringer then,
this last swim of the summer.
After a smear of Pietro's
espresso and brittle
bone-textured cone,
my hand shakes,
ice cream drips.

# Bait knife

Last night's force 5 has left Solva's fishermen
shipping extra hours in their beds,
but not Mikey, and me the pensioned apprentice,
boarding Helen C.

The diesel beast is defibrillated back to life,
coughs, clears its black lungs,
roars at the breaking dawn,
settles into a knock-knock-knock.

Moorings slipped into the harbour slick,
we turn out to the storm's back yard,
ruckus nearly done, tin cans kicked over,
sea running this way and that, cross as a crossed
    lover.

She hasn't forgotten who started all this
slaps us, shakes the boat, spits in my eye.
Pulls at my lapel,
*Why did you leave me? Do you care if I die?*

We haul our spoils, crabs, lobsters, conger eel.
The winch whines its recriminations,
weed garlanding landed creels,
boots braced against the bullying swell.

*You always take, you never give*
Raw wind rants in my ear
*Why on this sea should I let you live?*
Forces the stench of bait down my throat.

We snatch what the sea made shell –
biscuit sand, rock bed blue,
these tellers of prehistory soon to
blush in the boiler's rude breath.

# I have a hangover and the cat's vet
## is an Elvis fan

I have a hangover and the cat's vet is an Elvis fan.
His fingers force open the cat's jaws.
In the Elvis look-a-like competition he came third.
Mr Presley underwent his terminal event when he was
   on the commode.
His insides had compacted with a clay-like substance –
put so much pressure on his heart his aorta burst.

He shows me photos of fleas,
then gives the cat a shot of steroids
and me a tube of powder to dust my carpet.

At the reception desk I write a cheque
as the vet shapes an imaginary quiff in the mirror.

# Cat death

Swooning from the hypodermic's kiss
the tomcat slides down –
butter in a hot skillet.

His eyes bright with fear and betrayal,
a cat's instincts kick in.
He calls his body to claw for life.

But muscles, sinews have coalesced,
the coiled spring of a cat's will
collapsed in the toxic rush.

A cooling, cat-cushion.
The vet configures limbs
for that last run through the dark earth.

# My sister-in-law has new breasts

We travel to see them.
She greets us,
and I hold her closer than usual
to test their resilience – on the firm side.
They cost £3000 – or 1500 quid each.
She regards them as having separate identities.
She wears a tight halter top and in the pub,
practises resting them on the table.

# Ash

Axe arcing in crisp spring air.
The rhythm of this swing,
strike the log right and
cleaving is easy.

Until the blade hits knots
deflected by twisted grain,
hickory shaft shudders
and jumps with shock.

Branch to trunk
fibres interlock,
tested by wind, snow
the beating rain.

So here I am with
aching muscles,
stacking wood,
wondering at the history
of this tree.

Deep in winter's night,
flames don't know
what's new or old,
twisted or straight.
They roll and flicker
to grey after
the fire's story's told.

# Forget Coal

Forget coal, yea really forget coal
*(I've forgotten already – what is coal?)*
Forget zinc and tin and definitely steel.
Steel doesn't exist any more
not in Wales anyway.
Who cares – who needs it?
And while you are at it
forget washing machines
plane wings and slim-line TVs.
That's not the future.
That's not where Wales is.
It's not where Merthyr is.
Not even where Llanrwst is.
*(I've not put that in to rhyme with Proust.*
*That ain't where this is going.*
*We don't need any intellectual literary bullshit.*
*Not now, not any more)*

**The future**
It's all about big zins, big cabs
and big, big concepts...

Think
        Applets for a variety of emerging iPlatforms
Think
        Start-ups that provide hosting
        for micro-packages that skim information
        for cheese heads
Think
        Honking away on a widget that that will

fuse users' ganglia to the cortex of the
digital brain stem.

The business of Wales, is not business.
It's monetizing what is in our heads,
that leaves a lot of room for wusses
like me, and you too.

**_Get with the program!_**

# Indicators

I sit down with the boss.
This man who checks
my figures and figures out
if I add value to the business,
pay my way and carry
my share of the cost
of those, like him, who
spend their time checking
and producing evidence
as to whether I'm worth
employing or not.

He looks grim, thumbs
through a wad of papers,
*The Indicators –*
*(Turnover, Utilisation, Profitability)*
and says that there are now
*New Indicators –*
*(Value of Work Done,*
*Work in Progress, Uninvoiced Fee)*
These tell him that
since the last year
I have become
*Marginal.*

# Reds

I can wear red
Now that my mother
Is dead

When I was 20
She said
*Red clashes with your acne*

My desire to become
A revolutionary
So easily undone

Pushing 62
Your red-shirted son
Pays homage to you

And sad but true
I haven't read Trotsky
For years

# The hottest day

Today is the hottest day,
gritter lorries are out
to stop our roads melting away.

Water tankers are deployed,
transfer deals not closed;
the radio proffers stern advice –

*Don't open windows*
*Keep curtains drawn*
And in Kent they perform a rain dance every
    dawn.

The woman from the department is quizzed
*Should breast-fed babies drink water?*
*What happens if they stop breathing?*

Somewhere, somebody has been detected watering
    a lawn.
and will be incarcerated until the ice caps melt
which won't be long at this rate.

At the edge of the motorway on a bank
a makeshift awning is constructed
to shelter children from the sun's roar.

At night the house sighs
sounds and smells stream, hot sand
through a clenched hand.

The television man is blurred
by a haze of static,
his throat is thick with war.

# Autumn

In the morning he sweeps leaves
into the grieving wind,
they rattle in the rake's teeth.

He deals death in the afternoon,
pours poison,
grants absolution like a god.

His feet make cider.
Sucked soft by sweetness
the lanterns of juice collapse.

Damp moss licks the lawn,
green tongue flicking,
fungi feed on decay.

The terrorist wasp dies
against the setting sun,
a martyr to the lost cause of summer.

# Leathers

Another M4 slog
and I'm stretching my legs in Membury,
when this short bloke addresses me in Italian.

Then, in broken English,
he appeals to my compassion and greed.
Before I know it I've forked out 200 quid.

And four Versace Leathers,
still in their posh bags,
lie like corpses in the boot.

The rest of the day
I congratulate myself
on being a lucky bastard.

Later in the pub
I tell my story,
smell again the rich leather.

When my friend says
this sounds like something
On *Crimewatch* – even down to the Italian –

turns out that
the only thing leather
is the label *Handmade in Italy*.
The suede, the bomber,

three-quarter length and women's belted,
are plastic, liberally sprayed with eau de
    cowdologne.

I stand in front of the mirror.
My wife is checking the
The car boot sale date.

# Dinner Date

You are mixed up
with all the pornographic images
that float through my head
on a river of cheap whiskey.
Nights like these
the words of your songs
jump out of my ears
and dance around the room.

Tonight we were going to make love.
I'd set my mind on it,
the candlelit supper,
me across the table from you
fingers only just touching.
I would ask you how the CD was going,
did the new guitarist fit in,
what about your next concert?

You see I know how to woo a girl.
It's all about you.
But you didn't show.
So the steak is in the bin,
the wine is down the sink
and I'm here,
watching the Freeview –
trousers around my ankles.

# Freezer log

I chart the freezer's contents
in a list blu-tacked to the door:
the what, the when,
the how long it can be stored.

This mausoleum
of stars and ice and frost,
the drawers cracked on their runners
keeping cold the logged and lost.

The small nuggets of inspiration
packed in freezer bags –
hopes and minor ambitions
have lost their jam jar tags.

Next to the stiff flaps of pitas,
the reused frozen peas,
and the brittle, sullen lobster
marooned in a silent sea

are the big ideas,
the brilliant schemes,
the worldwide tours,
the wild-eyed dreams,

all coated in white indifference
unsentimental as rocks.
The freezer breathes, sighs,
shudders, mocks.

# First Bass

We have our introduction,
line zipping out of the reel –
a shaking of hands so to speak –
you somewhere deep
cursing the fascination
of a fatal, false attraction.

This is a first for me,
but I know to let you run,
hunting currents,
twisting with the tide
as the hook bites.

Rod handle kicking,
left fist locked,
my right hand ready to slip
more line. The wheel turns,
you tire;
breaking the surface
tail slapping.

Lying between my feet
your betrayed eyes die
blood runs cold in your gills:
scaled, spiked, spent.

# The funeral crowd

There are fewer of us now, of course.
In fact, for Stan's funeral we are down to six,
the rump of the old architect's department.
Me, the youngster, Pam the oldest.
She leans on my arm like my mother
only she is stick-thin, Jaeger-attired.
my mother was bigger – oh, and Pam is worth
    millions.

We are a happy crew.
We talk of only two things –
the old times and ailments.
The older you are the more ailments you have,
Pam dominates the conversation.
She's licked them:
breast cancer, spinal problems.
She is down to one good eye
and she's always been pretty deaf.
She's alive despite the medical establishment,
she's alive because she's Pam.
And the old times – we were all great then,
everybody else had been idiots.
The stories are the same
but even funnier for the telling.

My, isn't it the best feeling –
to be in a sharp black suit
at a funeral
on a sunny day in spring?

# Dare

I linger next to the ice cream van,
threaten the angelic horrors
as their tongues lap the cones.
*I believe in child slavery.*

I bite the neck of the woman
I'm standing next to in the lift
growl into her flesh
*Take me to Transylvania – now!*

I wander into the art gallery
reeking of petrol
carrying a flame thrower.
*There's a need for more spontaneity.*

I sprinkle talcum powder into an envelope,
and send it to the mayor
with the message
*Snort Anthrax sucker.*

I steer this car
into the queue at the bus stop.
My wipers beat away blood.
*Fuck.*

I stand up in the plane,
read pure fear in their faces.
*I've swallowed enough Semtex
to take us all down.*

If I had a powerful rifle,
and if my cross hairs
were fixed on your chest,
do you think I would hesitate
before I pulled the trigger?

# An ordinary woman

Death is its own mortician,
makes you look ten years younger
than the woman I met on ward F,
only a few days ago.

I was passing through,
it was not my domain.
You showed me old photographs –
a woman with her family:

husband soon to be broken on the hill
as you forced a farmer's living,
and children, like any children, now gone
to Canada, Australia, Hong Kong.

Llangadog, a couple with eager offspring.
That small bundle of cracked pictures
the key to your memories,
bound by an elastic band.

Now my knife begins the descent
through your flesh, I will know
your body better than your husband,
your children. Better even, than you.

Before I remove lungs to weight them,
before I take out the brain to apply my callipers,
before I uncoil jewelled intestines,
I wonder. What will I find?
Will there be Welshness through your spine?

A smell of gorse and heather in your spleen?
Hymns caught in your throat, blood spilling
forgotten recipes for *Teisen ar y maen?*

The procedures complete,
my assistant hoses the mortuary floor.
The death was unexceptional,
displaying nothing untoward.

# Calling time

We shuffle around the reception room.
Soundtrack, a generation's nightmare;
monitors loop footage of bulldozed bodies.

Our guide once led prisoners
down the stone steps, now
our lift descends in darkness.
It's a dramatic effect
*to enhance our visitor experience.*
He tells us that the last letters
these prisoners wrote were
torn up in their faces.

We are herded along
with no time to enter the cell
just big enough to stand in,
to press the walls of the padded room,
to trace a finger in the carved initials of the
    condemned man,
to touch the bulk of the hunched gallows.

The instruments of torture,
wire flex, rubber tubing,
we barely notice.
In the room of commemoration
the candles are put out.
It's 6pm.
The attendants have their families to go to.

# Doc Graham

Bent over his barber's chair,
hot wasps of needles
dining on my buttock,
Doc Graham mops red sweat.

Back after thirty years
four stops up Tudor Street,
I want that missing wing
to finish some unfinished business.

What have you been doing Doc,
all this time?
Your own tattoos are faded blue memories;
do you recall me, that drunk in the suit?

*I have scanned acres of skin*
*Swum in rainbow inks*
*Sailed swelling galleons of desire*
*Made knuckles of love and hate*
*Roared dragon masterpieces*
*Savage Maori war markings*
*Painted Popeye's anchor*
*I love you Mam*
*every girl you can think of in every possible*
    *place*

My butterfly
got buried under suit trousers
through too many 9 to 5s
squashed by the weight of the mortgage

and the arse of a business man.

Now
see how it flutters.
Wings are testing the air.

# Long Swell

Here in the middle of St Brides Bay
I shut my eyes; call of a gull,
distant surf from Newgale Beach,
human sound carried out
to me on the water is indecipherable.
Closer, moving through the kayak's
plastic intricacies, sea has its say.

The sun, unseasonably hot for May,
explores the difference between
wetsuit and skin; shadows of clouds shift,
after-images flare,
then the kayak turns away.

Sway of a long swell
moving from America, Ireland,
to crash onto Welsh sand.

A compass needle
I spin slowly.
Rhythms change, sounds move.
If I open my eyes
I will see a jellyfish
swimming the blue depths.

All this, just to get away from you.

## '60'

What a fine number 60 is.

I see you sitting by the fire
slippered, corpulent
your arms rest on the fat O
of your stomach,
distended from devouring
all those years.

Here's me
back wracked,
one-eyed,
body parts bottled in formaldehyde,
knees near knackered.
I'm not ready to join
you on the comfy chair;
So shift your arse,
get out of there.

# Blue Kite at Rest Bay

Air's ambition tamed by tubular ribs
parabola of taut fabric
strained filaments
control lines curved against clouds.

This man on the beach
a marionette,
feet planted firm
he dips and sways.

Like a yachtsman
he leans back
shoulder blades touch
not surf but sand.

As if on a spring
the kite lifts him,
wind in the bent wing
and the strings sing.

# The Trouble

When did the magic go?
When was it that I looked at your face
and you no longer set me on fire?

That's the trouble
with these long-distance relationships,
we didn't see enough of each other.

If I'm being honest
it was only one way.
Each time you sang

I thought it was only for me,
but then I saw through you –
you were playing the field,

the songs aren't great, and
the way you wore your hair
on *Never Mind the Buzzcocks*.

# The survivor

One newspaper describes me
as a cancer survivor,
so I become fair game
for confessions, revelations, fears.

One, with cysts on his testicles:
the other, make that two,
who worry about getting it on,
requesting techniques for cunnilingus;
one wants tips on childcare;
a worried man, cake icing.

> *I say don't worry*
> *It's always grim at 3am*
> *Test the pelvic floor*
> *Use good sugar*
> *Surgeons are heroes*
> *Or Sweeney Todd*
> *From nappies you came*
> *And to nappies you will return*

They are all grateful.
They make the sign of the cross,
say *Christ*.

# Budgerigar

Age is inexorable.
Just take last week
I went shopping with my son
and walked into a large mirror.
Worse than that
I apologised to the man I bumped into.
Worse than that
I thought how rough the old guy looked.

# Early morning running

Behind me night lies in ruins
on to the blind summit bandaged in gauze

heart plays bass
to the riff in my veins

trespass over golf club greens
kick jewels from a par four

I'm out-running the moon
as it slides from the sky

exhausted from hosting
another wild night on the mountain

coaxing fungi out of folds of mould
getting amongst the badger's set

howling at the farmer's dog
playing Bonnie to Reynard's Clyde

my feet rattle rocks
in a dry stream bed

into this smashed bowl
of the time-lost quarry

yellow light bounces with echoes
last breath of a breeze

crows, fragments of funeral cloth,
flit in and out of fissures

rest and rise from ledges
hover in the morning thermals

a Tesco trolley caught in mid-air
the city snapping at my heels

# Before the big run

Look, said the chiropractor,
even your feet are the wrong shape
– arches too high, toes
pointing in the wrong direction.

My ballet dancer's points
have turned into raptor talons
rhino-tough toenails.
Bones hastily assembled
as if God were at the end of an exam,
just wishing
to get this question out of the way
in the time that was still available.

# We meet again

Why is it always the same?
I think I'm over you
then you come out of nowhere –
like here in Morrisons,
me getting my octopus skinned.

I have deleted you from
my screensaver,
erased you from my favourites.
You didn't DM my tweets.
We were going nowhere.

You sound as if
you slipped in here
in your pyjamas and slippers
grabbing a pack of Silk Cut,
sliced bread, carton of milk.

# Another Jug

*The first love hurt, that was the worst. She was the big one; I'll never feel for a woman like that again. When my wife left it was OK, except financially of course: she screwed me to the wall. I had to buy myself out of the long-term commitment to her, re-mortgage the house. Now she drives her boyfriend around in a Volkswagen Touareg – MY Touareg, my money bought it.*

I've just ordered another jug, this is the one that in the morning he will say, if only you hadn't bought the last jug. He continues: *that woman, I was crazy about her. The sort of love that makes you cut people up, lie and steal for. We had a daughter I haven't seen her for nearly twenty years.* He looked at his palm as if his mobile nestled there. *I know the number, I could dial it now, after all these years.* His gaze switches to the stage. The three Philippina singers are launching into Achy-breaky-heart. That one, he says. *Face like a young Diana Ross, hair touched with a tarbrush, body tight as a drum, legs that don't seem right close together. She's my dream.*

Effrin Montez and the A-live Band finish their set. A record plays over the sound system. *Money can buy you a fine dog, only love can make it wag its tail.*

I order another jug.

# Here

Here is where I saw you first
in your blue handmade suit with
a butcher's stripe,
the girl I would marry.

Here is where we made love
in the early morning light
and conceived
our first-born.

Here is where we stood,
and you cried for
all that was lost
and thrown away.

Here is where we wondered
at the future, how
it came to us and how,
too soon, it disappears.

Here, here in the darkness
I never tire of the telling
braille of bodies
breath on skin.
Let another chapter begin.

# Damning with high praise

He is to introduce her.
She is a famous poet,
He is not.
She has a low opinion of him
He of her.
Should he damn with faint praise?
No, not on your life.
He says that she is the greatest poet
Since Byron, Shelley, Ted Hughes and his wife.
The reputation of the laureate is not secure.

Never have words chimed so sublimely
As under her flowing pen
A poetic coming so timely –
Surely the greatest poet in the land.

Ladies and gentlemen:
Please give a big hand.

Everybody agreed
The reading did not live up to the introduction.

# Without Words

My words will not come out to play anymore
they plead overwork, stress, exhaustion
sit around in my skull, smoking and lolling about.

I say – hey, come on, let's crank out some doggerel
like the good old days,
try rhyme, a sonnet, limericks, Haiku,
ramble around free verse.

The words look askance
if body language could scream,
I'd be deafened by *Fuck You.*

Even my favourite words
stare back insolently,
accuse me of abuse

making them flog their guts out in dry reports,
nonsensical emails, letters so formal as not to need
    words
but barbed wire, guns, concrete.

I confront a blank screen
then over my shoulder I hear them tittering
now laughing out loud –
these words are having the best fun they have had in
                                                    ages.

# Poem from nowhere

This poem came to me
In the half-consciousness of waking.
Perfectly formed, complete.
I marvelled at its simplicity, neatness.
It scanned, had its own rhythms,
Culminated in the perfect last line.
The understatement made me smile.
Even the title was good.
In writing it down, however,
It turned out like this.

# Knee high

I'm in a television studio
filming a programme
that no one will see
because it's OnDigital

Nadeira interviews me
this woman is beautiful
beyond television dreams
dark skin and eyes

glossy black hair falling
over a faux fur collar
framing her flawless chest
the stools however

are studio chic
uncomfortable to sit on
and by an ergonomic quirk
it is impossible to cross your legs

I hear the producer's voice
whispering in the shell
of Nadeira's earpiece
telling her to close her legs

as the camera snout
is getting a lensfull
Nadeira's thighs clamp tight
the brightness of her smile

does not dim
when she laughs
she forgets the injunction
rocks on the Styrofoam toadstool

her legs falling apart
over its slippery edges
I have to deliver
my poem standing up

peering into the dark
at the studio's fringe
the cameras pointing
elsewhere.

# Everyman

There is no publicity.
The organiser arrives late.
There are five readers and the MC, Nathan,
who reads more poems than the readers.

George and Sarah, a conscript,
are the audience.
Later, a third arrives,
who is drunk and
takes issue with the poems as they are being read.
She will fall over spectacularly when she leaves.

So, really, only George is the audience.
He takes his responsibilities seriously,
smiling frequently and inappropriately.

Ian tells me that the average audience
for a poetry reading is eight.
And more people go to art galleries
than football matches.

We drink, return to our hotel.
The room is defiantly non-ensuite.

The next day I go to an art gallery.

The following week the organiser will ask
for the reading fee to be refunded.

# Travis

Lee Harwood confides in us,
his poetry-loving audience,
a long held secret –
his first name is Travis.

The only Travis I've come across
is Bickle, and I cannot imagine
Harwood driving a taxi,
getting involved in a gunfight.

Although, if you are asking,
being read his poems
while bleeding to death
would ease the passing.

# Second Life

I am sending you, Lucia, my alter ego
out into the world to avenge me,
to destroy my former lover just
as he tried to destroy me.

My Second Life avatar:
composite of the most beautiful
women in the world, Facebook
construct more alive than me.

See how he reads Lucia's texts –
those intimate pornographic
missives that implore him to return
from China, trade electronic pulses.

His replies, one hundred in one day
litter my phone, hot and impatient
he cannot wait to be with her.
Blinded by lust, he didn't realise

he was being duped.
But would you really meet a goddess
in a café
in Crouch End?

# Torrance

Room 246 for the first time:
the walls are concrete block,
a fluorescent light buzzes,
chairs, tables are prison basic –
hardly appropriate for creativity.
On my left a fellow novice writes:

> *I rip out the cheque*
> *An alarm call to a dream*

On the other side of the table,

> *The orchard field*
> *Is thick with windfalls*
> *My feet make wine*

I write nothing.
I didn't think it would be like this.

Torrance for example –
trousers tucked into boots,
old coat, weather-beaten face.
Surely he's not a writer
not The Tutor.
He looks like a mountaineer,
no, with the rucksack, a Sherpa,
eyes bright, sharp as a hawk.

Then Torrance talks,
he pulls me in.

We made a few climbs that year.
Torrance the Sherpa.
Sharing the load.
Pointing the way.

# Torrance at 70

Torrance looks like a tortoise.
He is seventy, and we are here
to celebrate his life and
listen to Lee Harwood.

Torrance mounts the stage.
At the lectern, his head pops out
from the over-large white suit,
his face is brown and beaked.

He snaps off words as if
eating celery.

# After the poetry reading

We were not invited back to the organiser's house;
he is rich and a poetry devotee, so that explains it.
So we reminisce. He recalls, vividly, Jackie's tight
leather trousers, red shirt, no bra. I remember.
She shone. And the other woman who claimed he
stalked her, said he was possessed,  called up his
friends to complain; I know, I was one of them. Well,
he said, she phoned me by mistake, just recently.
After the swearing she was quite civil, does pottery.

# Giving advice

I play the elder statesman to this young poet
give her the benefit of my long experience.
Ah, yes, the Tunnel Club with Malcolm Hardee –
that was a tough gig, but Hay, what a doddle.

You have got to give something back, I think,
conveniently forgetting to mention that all that
was 30 years ago and since then a blank.
She looks at me, her smile pleasant, enquiring.

As her train pulls in she stands to leave
thanks me for the good advice.
It dawns on me what she's really thinking,
*This guy's a fucking twat.*

# The reading fee

He wants to give me the fee
for the reading I have not done.
His fingers sift through his wallet:
five twenties for 15 minutes.

He is pressing money
into the hand that did not gesticulate
nor turn pages; me saying no
with the mouth that did not recite

to the audience that even now
is moving into the dining room
where I would have been eating.
I hear laughter and chatter.

I decline the fee.
I have not read.
And having not sung,
I do not get my supper.

The money is back in his wallet,
the fat hinge of leather shuts.
It slides tight into the inside pocket
of his Paul Smith suit.

The poems
fly around my head.

# Autumn beach

Soon this beach will be mine again.
Those September stragglers
back in their cities,
sand washed from their hair.

The lifeguard,
no longer keeps vigil from his hut,
his flags have been
surrendered to the sea.

The invaders' tented village
gone and the pub sign all ensuite
will creak as a chill wind
chases the chip papers.

I walk the sands ridged as the roof
of a mouth wide with joy;
gulls call goodbye, goodbye,
to the last cars climbing the hill.

I turn to the waves
*Just you and me.*

# Writing the bid

Our corporate pass cards
wrapped in blue neck cord
on the table next to car keys.
We sit in this room,
writing the bid,
looking at each other
over open laptops.

The bid-leader's words –
*What is <u>the story</u>?*
*Say we are <u>integrated</u>.*
*Say we are <u>flexible, responsive.</u>*
*Demonstrate our <u>can-do philosophy</u>.*
*<u>Unfurl</u> the banner, <u>weave the golden thread</u>.*

The memory stick passes between us.

The blinds stay shut.
The heating comes on.
The room overheats.
Outside our glass wall
office workers arrive,
work, talk, eat, leave.

The drafts come back,
obliterated in track changes.
The room is getting cold.
I hear the security man
coming down the corridor.

*There is no story.*
*We have disintegrated*
*We are rigid and unresponsive*
*Our philosophy is no-can-do*
*The banner is frayed and we have lost the golden*
  *thread.*
*(in fact we never had it in the first place)*

# Caroline Street

The divide:
Brewery Quarter –
a brash ¼ quarter
kitted out
in building designer gear,
glossed in structural glass
and orange rendered panels
windows eyelined in grey steel
balconies jutting
like a young slapper's tits.
Signature architecture.

This lot looks down on the
clapped-out south side
Dorothy's Fish Bar,
Tony's, the kebab and burger bars –
that feel the sharp elbows
of the new kid in town.

*(Wasn't old man brewery
carted off because the smell of hops
clinging to his coat blistered
Chanel like paint stripper)*

In the day these old buildings skulk,
shuffle feet on cracked paving stones,
daylight burns their eyes.
Come Saturday midnight,
a tide roars through
Strait Caroline.

The old fast food joints
provide the chips, gristle and grease
that pours into the gullets of the good
    timers.
A flotsam of food wrapping
slops and swirls ankle-deep.
Lads on the lash take a piss
on the Brewery Quarter wall
hell, they know which side of the street
their bread is buttered.
On to Life, OZ, Oxygen, Sam's –
Cardiff nights fuelled by Caroline Street.

# Sext

*This love will never end.*
Her closing words ever time she phoned
sharing the details of her day,
other more tantalising intimacies.

We played at dirty phone sex.
*Let me hear the zip of your flies.*
*Close your eyes.*
*Imagine your hand parting my thighs.*

I speed dial, listen to her voicemail.
*Tell me in two words*
*what you were going to tell me in a thousand...*
I imagine the dip of her blouse,
the rustle of her skirt.

I contemplate
her blurred, erotic image.
*Send.*

# Urban cockerel

I don't hear you through
Argon filled double-glazing
in the cocoon of my
housing estate home.

The warm autumn has prised open
my windows, and this morning
your call awakened me:
an urban cockerel.

Cock of the walk in Crystal Glen –
not quite the farmyard of your ancestors,
not quite that empire of animals,
not quite the need to maintain the pecking order.

I haven't seen your coop.
I imagine a cock in straitened
circumstances, taking an apartment
here in the city, with just the one hen.

In these times of financial uncertainty,
credit crunch and diminished pensions,
it's difficult to maintain a country residence –
better to slum it here, in social housing.

If she manages a couple of eggs a day,
it will be enough to keep the bailiffs away.
Enough to see you through.
So cock-a-doodle-do to you too.

# Bay Sailing

Lord Bute built the docks.
His engineer was McConnochie
Who illustrated the usual paradox.
He chose not to live here by the sea,
In terraces of Georgian splendour,
But up in town where
He hobnobbed with the gentry.
It paid off. They made him mayor.
Arms-length progress.

The muddy waters of the Bay
Need constant aeration.
Costing Cardiff £700 per day
To avoid weeds and stagnation.
Why are we prepared to pay so much?
You could say we were conned by
The politics of the murky pond.
Was that progress?

In the Norwegian church we've got,
As judged by Professor Parry,
The worst building of the lot.
And that probably includes the docks of Barry.
But the NCM is an architectural thrill,
Clad in polished granite from Brazil,
Looking like a liner underway,
Designed by HMA.
Definitely progress.

The Pierhead Building by William Frame
Welcomed home our sailor boys
And deserves its fame.
Built in 1896 with chimneys, and gargoyles
It is a masterpiece of French Gothic.
The motto *Wwrth Ddwr a Than*
Reminds us how the elements
Forged industrial man
And Wales.

Rocco Forte built a five-star hotel,
Topped by a pterodactyl,
Menus by Marco-Pierre White,
Who foodies reckon is all right,
If you don't mind paying through the nose
For little salads and foodie cameos,
Mind you chips and a Clark's pie
Is better than a poke in the eye
In Caroline Street.

Pause a moment in West Bute Street
Built in 1927 – the NatWest Bank,
Marvel at this architectural feat.
We've got none other than Vitruvius to thank
For these fluted Ionic columns
Doorway surmounted by a bronze of Equity.
Though the dockers would hardly agree
Fate didn't deal even-handedly
With the people of Tiger Bay.
Iron master Crawshay gave to the rich
What he took from the poor.
On the line of what was once a ditch.
He dug the Glamorganshire Canal in 1794;

Barges carried iron or coal to the sea.
The words on his grave *God Forgive Me*
Are those of a man full of regret?
More like one who was hedging his bets.
Canal and man are buried now.

Lord Bute would never know
A day when the tide didn't ebb and flow.
Now there will be no more summer nights,
Sitting on the Red House wall,
Watching the flicker of docklights
As the water level begins to fall,
No more mornings hearing dunlin call.
Instead there's the buzz of it all.
You can drown in cappuccino.

Still, let's be realistic.
It's easy to get nostalgic
for what never existed.
So which way now?
John Clinch's *People like Us*
points towards the Bosphorus,
dog sniffing the air.
So perhaps we should share
The animal's sense of anticipation.
I do.

# Uniform

I waited for you on our first date.
You arrived dressed in faded denim
armed with flowers, you joked,
*sometimes it's good to come late.*

In the church, of course, it was you,
dressed in soldier's red and blue,
who had to wait for me.
We declared a truce.

For a man of action,
you loved to stay in bed.
It was the smell and warmth of me
that kept you there, you said.

Now you are home early.
I stand in church where we once stood.
Your six best friends are with you,
your uniform is polished wood.

# Wedding Year

Dan and I on the cliff path run,
late afternoon in January,
chasing the setting sun.

You testing me,
the booming bell of my heart
rocking in the chest's cathedral,
ringing out over Nine Wells –
those Iron Age ramparts,
on to Caerfai Bay.
Turning at Twr y Felin you say
*Go faster, go faster*
*don't slow down to run uphill*

Family roots go deep here.
They jostle with those of gorse, sea pinks,
and share Syr Benfro's soil.
From Solva to St Davids
your bridal path with Laura
my bridal path with Gill.

Nearly home, running alone
through Llanunwas.
The slap of feet on tarmac,
running to memory's metronome.
Headlights of a car
turn me into a movie star –
either that or roadkill.

At Panteg Road
I close on your shoulder.
We are here
at Nant yr Ardd,
at the beginning
of this wedding year.

# The bride

and she shines
the bride shines with the sun
her white her gold
we watch as she enters the church
we gasp we ooh we ahh
and the hymns *Guide me, Guide me,*
so light the *Song of Solomon*
the words the singing
the beauty the tears welling
but always the bride
she shines brighter
the wedding bells peel
the words spill we say he says,
the bride's father – her beauty
her taking the last sweet
from her sister
we laugh the little girl
the beginning he was there
and her mother she tilts her head
bright eyed as a blackbird
we rising the champagne,
the bubbles bursting and rising again
we toast the bride the bride
we all say yes the bride
and the groom how was he chosen?
why him he queries why him why her?
but the answers are in her eyes
in her smiles
and we dance and she moves

and she laughs
the bride
the bride

# Truest love

I will feed you, my lover,
until you are too fat
to fuck another.

> *I will rub onions*
> *into your hair*

> *Place chilli seeds*
> *in the folds of your foreskin*

> *Garland the cleft of your buttocks*
> *with crushed garlic*

> *Fill your cheeks*
> *with red ants' eggs*

> *Blow opium smoke*
> *into your lungs*

> *Hang vampire bats*
> *from your earlobes*

> *Coil a tiger snake*
> *in your skull*

Do not betray me, my lover,
or I will make sure
you never fuck another.

# For Kitty and Vince's Diamond Wedding

In that first year after war,
love light as paper,
Kitty and Vince shone like diamonds
in Neath's Victoria Gardens.

She wore cotton on her shoulders
and he wore leather on his runner's feet.
They strode together in marriage.
Welsh flowers in a London street.

In their 10th year tin from Trostre.
Tinplate works, alloy, made of each
other, shaped to a purpose,
coiled in each other's arms.

They were as strong as Port Talbot steel,
gathering Conway pearls to the 20th year.
Kitty as beautiful as Nantgarw porcelain
glazed and painted with the Vale of Neath.

Then, at 40, *win coch*:
A Welsh rugby shirt, blood and rubies,
and the flushed cheeks of a walk
with Gwyneth and Ifor to happy Gilfach Goch.

Gwynfynedd burnished gold
by 50 autumn leaves:
Life turning like a wedding band
On the fine skin of a finger.

Today, as the sea scatters
jewels of spray in Rest Bay,
we celebrate this diamond –
the marriage of Kitty and Vince.

# Fall guy for Erin

Today I'm her best friend.
We have made ourselves invisible
in Edgbaston's Botanical Gardens.
We have found the energy seat
behind the bamboo screen,
and we are fully charged and ready
to hunt pirates and robbers who come
disguised as old women in wheelchairs
or brides in parrot-red saris.

We are not fooled, we know the
Blood dogs will be hunting us soon,
so we rub ourselves with rosemary and mint
move through the grass like jaguars
or roll down long grass lawns,
runaway logs in a blur.

She spins on the end of my arms
*higher, faster, more, more*
If I let go now she will fly to the stars.
I am giddy with joy, but it won't last.

When we get home, and the grown-ups
check her for cuts and bruises,
it will be me that she blames.
I will be her all-too-visible fall guy.

# Paloma

It's over now.
I've met somebody else.
It's not you,
it's me,
but it's you
too.
She's dressed in a body stocking,
decorated with a road map to my heart.
She's going to make me dance *kerching, kerching*.

# Author Notes

Ifor Thomas' last book of poetry *Body Beautiful* was shortlisted for the Wales Book of the Year. He has performed his poetry throughout Wales and England at venues as diverse as the Tunnel Club in London and the Hay Literary Festival. He has won the John Tripp Award for Spoken Poetry. He has a long connection with the Welsh literary community.

His fiction has been broadcast on Radio 4 and he has won the British Airways Travel Writer of the Year Award.

Ifor Thomas was born in Pembrokeshire in 1949. He trained as an architect in London and Cardiff, where he lives. He worked for many years in the National Health Service, involved with the design and construction of health buildings.

# Acknowledgements

Some of these poems, or versions of these poems, have appeared in the magazines Poetry Wales, New Welsh Review, Yellow Crane, Red Poet, Square. *Caroline Street* appeared in the Big Book of Cardiff anthology edited by Peter Finch and Grahame Davies. *Dare* appeared in the on-line anthology 100 Poets Against the War Redux. *'60'* was written for a poetry event that took place at the top of Pen y Fan.

*What to say when criticising poetry*, and *Damning with high praise* appeared in the anthology Short Fuse: The Global Anthology of New Fusion Poetry edited by Todd Swift and Philip Norton. *The 100 Birds of Wales* was written for the Chapters music/word event held at Chapter, Cardiff in June 2010.

I would like to thank Kathryn Gray for her heroics in editing the manuscript.

# Reviews of *Body Beautiful*

'...a collection which can lay claim to this rather rare
poetic status: it is a real page-turner.'
MATTHEW JARVIS, *Planet*

'this book is not just memorable for the urgency of its
subject matter, the author's lively response to his brush
with mortality is what is most human and moves us.'
AMY WACK, *Poetry Wales*

'... In Ifor Thomas we have a real 21st Century voice; a
voice that can make itself heard above the roar of traffic
and the voices of kids as they come out of school. Ifor's
is the kind of poetic voice we need in these loud times.
Listen to it. Listen to it now...'
IAN MACMILLAN

'...With a superb sense of timing, Ifor Thomas grafts his
expertise in performance poetry onto sharper, leaner,
new work...the poems remain suffused with a gutsy
tenderness and compassion...'
GRAHAME DAVIES

# PARTHIAN

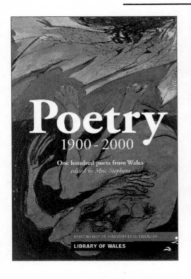

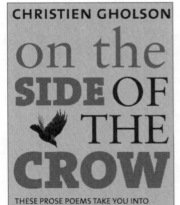

www.parthianbooks.com